LISTEN!

Can · Make · and · Do Books

LISTEN!

76 Listening Experiences for Children, Including 60 Rhythm and Musical Instruments to Make and Use

by Joy Wilt
Terre Watson

Photography by John Hurn

CREATIVE RESOURCES
Waco, Texas

Acknowledgments

I would like to express my gratitude to some very special people in my life. Their patience and reassurance made this book a pleasure to create.

A Giant Thank You to: my husband, Bill
my editor, Bruce Wilt
my photographer, John Hurn
my mother, Melena Edmonston
my neighbor, Bill Mullaney
my helpers, Jeff and Kristy
Wheeler and Emily Losey

TERRE WATSON

My thanks are added in equal measure to all the special people who helped make this book come to life. I am grateful for each and every one of you.

JOY WILT

Contents

III. MUSICAL INSTRUMENTS

The Importance of Sensory Experiences

This book is one of a series of four books about SENSORY EXPERIENCES FOR CHILDREN. This book deals with LISTENING experiences, while the other three books deal with:

TACTILE experiences
VISUAL experiences
TASTING AND SMELLING experiences.

We have chosen to devote four entire books to sensory experience because we feel that these experiences for children are very important.

Why are sensory experiences so important?
Because *ALL LEARNING AND COMMUNICATION BEGINS WITH SENSORY EXPERIENCES*.

A child is born "fully equipped" with a set of "natural tools"—the senses of sound, touch, sight, taste, and smell. These tools enable him to explore and discover the world of which he is a part. Exploration and discovery are vital to a child's life because they lead him into growth and development.

Each of the four sensory experience books is packed full of suggested experiences—experiences that are designed to

—assist a child in becoming *aware* of his senses
—encourage a child to develop his senses

—give a child the opportunity to begin using his
    senses as tools to answer his questions and *edu-
    cate* himself
—allow a child to *enjoy* life through his senses.

The sensory experiences that we recommend can be the
exciting beginning of a child's understanding and en-
joyment of his world. They can be the foundation for
every learning experience the child will ever encounter.
They can make learning a relevant part of every child's
life.

This is why we believe that sensory experiences in gen-
eral should not be an "optional part" of any program.
Indeed, they should be an integral part.

The particular experiences that we have chosen have
been tested and found to be successful with
    —infants
    —toddlers
    —preschoolers
    —children 6–12 years of age

Each experience can be adapted to fit into any situation
at
    —home
    —school
    —church
    —social functions
    —recreational programs

Each sensory experience can be experienced by an individual child or by a group of children.

No matter what particular sensory experience is used, how it is used, or where it is used, it has great potential for bringing children of all ages in touch with themselves and their world.

About Listening Experiences

This book specializes in listening experiences for children.

We consider listening to be a valuable part of a child's life because of the vital role it plays in communication. Listening makes it possible for a child to receive the sound communications that enhance his survival, growth and education. Listening usually precedes the child's understanding of words and his ability to say them. Thus, for those children who are physiologically able, listening is extremely important.

The experiences in this book are designed to
—assist the child in becoming aware of his sense
of hearing

—develop the child's listening skills to the degree
  that he is able to
        identify sounds
          distinguish one sound from another
            adapt sounds to his lifestyle and mode
            of communication

A special section in this book is devoted to rhythm instruments that can be made and used by children of all ages. These instruments can be used as sound devices as well as rhythm instruments. When used as rhythm instruments, they are sure to contribute greatly to a child's musical experience through increased participation and involvement in music. The more a child becomes involved in an activity the more he will gain from it.

  —Rhythm instruments make a child's experience
    with music *active* rather than *passive*.
  —Rhythm instruments make music *fun* for a
    child.
  —Rhythm instruments allow a child to *express*
    music in a way that is meaningful to him.

We sincerely hope that you and your children will enjoy exploring the "world of sound" as much as we have enjoyed putting this book together.

                              JOY WILT

Listening Experiences and Games

String-a-Ling

1. With the hammer and nail, poke a hole in the bottom of each can. Thread the string through the bottom of each can so that the open ends are facing out. Tie a knot at each end of the string.

You will need: 2 *empty cans or paper cups*
Nail
Hammer
15–20 feet of string

2. Two children are needed to use the String-A-Ling. Each child takes a can and walks away from the other until the string is taut. Have them take turns holding the can to their ear to hear or to their mouth to speak while their partner does the opposite.

Tube Telephone

1. Remove the fittings from the ends of the hose with the kitchen knife. Insert the funnels into each end of the hose and tape them in place. Have the children take turns holding the funnel to their ear to listen or to their mouth to speak as their partner does the opposite. The tube telephone may be taken from one room to the next, upstairs to downstairs, around the garage or house with a partner on each end.

You will need: 1 *25-foot garden hose*
                          2 *funnels*
                             Kitchen knife
                             Masking tape

2. A vacuum cleaner hose will produce a ready-made telephone. This is great to use around corners. One child can speak directly into the hose while the other one puts the open end to his ear and listens.

Sound Cans

1. Fill the cartons with various materials from the list above. Two cans filled with the same materials are needed so they will produce identical sounds. Tape the lids shut.

2. Cut out several large paper circles (approximately 10″ in diameter). You will need one circle for every two cartons.

You will need: 6 or more empty potato chip cans
2 sets each: ½ cup corn, ½ cup salt, 3 small rocks, 3 bells, 2 erasers, etc.

Masking tape
Paper
Scissors

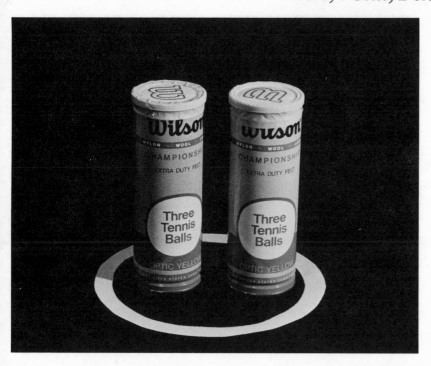

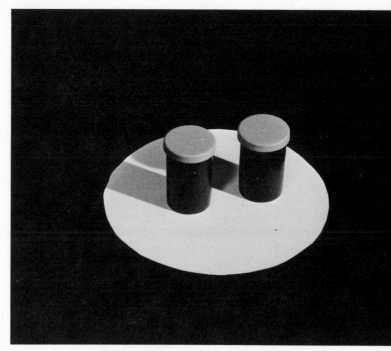

3. To use, mix up the various cartons on the table or floor. Have the child shake the cartons to identify the sounds, then put the two cans with the same sounds on the same large circle.

4. For variation, tennis ball cans, milk cartons, or small plastic film containers can be used to make the sound cans.

19

Twirly Hose

1. Use the knife to cut the garden hose into different-size pieces: a 3-foot length, a 5-foot length, and a 7-foot length. Have the child take one piece of hose at a time and twirl it over his head and listen to the sound it produces.

You will need: *Old garden hose which*
may be cut up
Kitchen knife

2. Have him repeat this with the other
lengths and compare the type of sound
heard each time. As variation, use different lengths of rope. Listen for the
different sounds they make when
twirled above one's head.

Humming Button

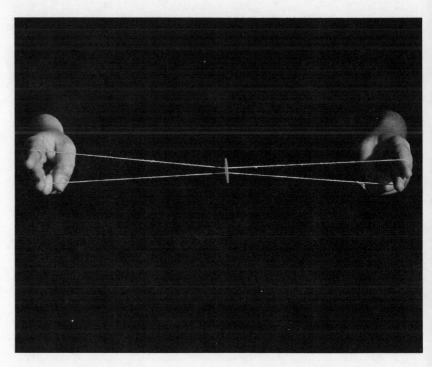

1. Thread the string through both holes of the button and tie the ends of the string together. Have the child place one hand into each loop of string. Then place the button in the center and hold the loops of string loose.

You will need: *1 button with 2 holes*
1 3′ piece of string

2. With both hands make a circular motion, so the button winds up the string. When the string is wound tightly, spread hands apart quickly. The button will spin rapidly and rewind the strings in the opposite direction. Continue with a gently spreading motion and listen to the humming. This becomes louder the closer the humming button is moved towards the ear.

Variation: For a softer humming sound, use a circular piece of cardboard instead of the button.

Spoon Sound Conductor

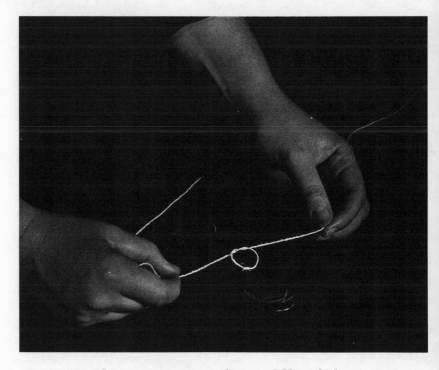

1. Tie the teaspoon to the middle of the string.

You will need: *1   stainless steel teaspoon*
                          1   3′ piece of string

2. Put the ends of the string up to your ears. Have a friend hit the teaspoon with various objects (other spoons, wood, erasers, metal, cloth, etc.) and listen to the sound travel up the string, noting the differences in the sounds. A fork, a larger spoon or a knife in place of the teaspoon will produce different sounds.

Echo Chambers

You will need: *Shower stall*
Closet
Large trash can
Oatmeal box
Bucket

1. When using the shower stall, closet, or large enough containers, have the child put his head inside and then make noises. When the small containers are used, have him talk into them. Listen for the echoes these containers will produce.

Soft or Loud?

You will need:

10	safety pins
10	pieces of macaroni
10	bottle caps
10	keys
5	books

1	crumpled piece of paper
1	block of wood
1	rock
1	chalk eraser

String
Blindfold

1. Fasten all but one of the safety pins together. Thread all but one of the pieces of macaroni onto a piece of string and fasten securely. Do the same with all but one bottle cap and with all but one key. Stack four of the books into a pile. You will now have a group of safety pins and a single safety pin; a group of macaroni pieces and a single piece of macaroni; a group of keys and a single key; a group of bottle caps and a single bottle cap; and a group of books and a single book. These will be used to create soft and loud noises by dropping onto a table or the floor.

2. Blindfold the child or turn him away so he cannot see what is being dropped. Ask him to listen for the loudest or softest noise (depending on concept being taught). Drop a single object or group at a time and have the child tell you which sounds are louder and which are softer.

Variation: A group of children could be divided into teams. Each team alternates players to guess at the answer. A point is scored for every correct answer.

High or Low?

You will need: *Piano, xylophone, guitar, or autoharp*
Box of assorted rhythm instruments: drums, shakers,
whistles, horns, bells, sticks, etc.

1. Help the children learn the difference between high and low pitches by giving examples and telling what they are. For example, hit the top and bottom keys on a piano one at a time and explain which is the high note and which is the low note.

2. Have the children take turns playing each of the instruments listed above to produce high or low notes. Have them tell you whether the pitches they have produced are high or low. It is also fun to guess before the instrument is heard if it will produce a high note or a low note.

Variation: High and low pitches can also be made with voices. Allow each child a chance to share his high voice and his low voice with the class.

Where Is That Noise Coming From?

You will need: One object which can make a sound (whistle, horn, or an instrument, etc.)
If none of these are available, use hand-clapping or your speaking voice

1. Have the children sit in a circle with their eyes closed.

2. The teacher or another child walks around the circle and stops where he wants the sound to come from.

3. The teacher or child then makes a sound with the object. Each one in the entire group then points in the direction from which he thinks the sound came.

29

What Is That Noise?

You will need: *Familiar classroom noises: toys that make noises, chairs, doors, instruments, animal-sound cans, activities that have a distinctive sound*
1 large oven or refrigerator carton or a table, turned on its side

1. Put the sound-producing materials behind the box or table. Have one child get behind the box or table and make a sound with one of the items from above.

2. Ask another child to guess what is making the noise.

3. Give each child an opportunity to make a sound behind the box.

Are These Noises The Same or Different?

You will need:

1 cardboard carton	10 bottle caps
1 coffee or tennis ball can	10 bells
1 plastic container	20 birthday candles
1 medium glass jar wrapped in masking tape	20 paper clips
1 jewelry or small box	1¼ cup corn kernels

1. This game is played in as many parts as there are objects. We have suggested five, but there are many more common objects that can be used.

   a. Put two bottle caps into each container. Have the children shake each container and observe the sound produced by each.

   b. Remove the bottle caps and then put two bells into each container. Shake the containers one by one. Do they sound the same or different from each other? From the bottle caps?

   c. Repeat the process, this time putting four birthday candles into each container and observing the different sounds produced.

   d. Put four paper clips into each container and observe the different sounds produced.

   e. Put ¼ cup of corn kernels into each container and observe the different sounds produced.

2. Before each container is shaken, the children may want to guess whether the sound will be the same as or different from the one they have just heard.

Sneaky Sound Game

You will need: 1 chair   Keys on a chain
1 blindfold   1 horn
1 bell   2 sticks
1 rattle

1. Have one child put on a blindfold and sit in a chair. Place the bell, rattle, keys, horn and two sticks below the chair.

2. Have another child start to crawl towards the chair. If the blindfolded child hears the child crawling towards the chair, he says, "I hear you," and the two children change places.

3. So long as the blindfolded child does not hear him, the other child continues to crawl. If he reaches the chair, he takes an object from under the chair and makes a noise with it.

4. The blindfolded child then guesses what object produced the noise.

Listening Comprehension

You will need: *Story or poem with several words (usually nouns) changed so as to create obvious errors*

Read the following story, or another, substituting wrong words for the right ones. When the children hear the wrong words they say "No" and give the right answer.

Every morning our friend Sarah got out of bed and put on her *pajamas* (clothes). She went into the bathroom and brushed her *face* (hair). She also would wash her *shoes* (face). When she was finished she walked down the *door* (stairs) to say good *night* (morning) to her parents. She pulled out a chair and sat down at the *bathtub* (table) to eat her breakfast. Sarah poured the milk into the *table* (bowl) and ate her cereal. She thanked her mother for breakfast. She then went to the door, turned the knob and walked out the *window* (door) to play.

Cassette Tapes

You will need: *Cassette tape*
Cassette recorder

1. Record familiar noises on a tape, leaving long enough intervals of silence between them so children have time to guess what the sounds are. Examples of some sounds that might be used are: trains, cars, motorcycles, buses, horns, airplanes, fire engines, tractors, cats, dogs, horses, cows, ocean, rain, thunder, running water, washing machine, clock, radio, lawn mower, etc.

2. You might also record familiar voices of children and adults. Have the children guess whose voice they are listening to.

Music and Feelings

You will need: *Liquid starch*
Dry powdered paint (non-toxic)
Paper
Record player
Assortment of records—jazz, classical, pop, lullabys, etc.

1. Each child should have a piece of paper with two teaspoons of starch and one teaspoon of powdered paint.

2. The children blend the two together by finger painting.

3. Play the various records for the children and watch the difference in the style of their finger painting.

Variation: Use the music this time for creative body movement. Play the various records for the children and watch how the style of their body movement changes.

Rhythm Instruments

Paper Rhythm Sticks

1. Roll up each piece of paper into a long tube.

You will need: *2 pieces of 8½″ x 11″ paper*

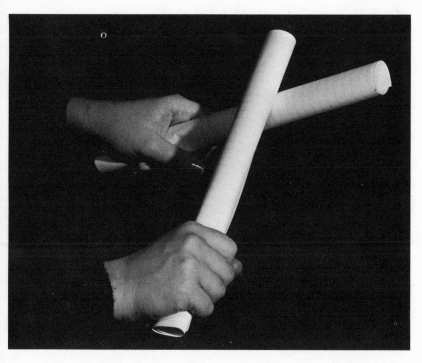

2. Have the children hit them together.
Ask them to describe the sound. Is it
soft or loud, gentle or noisy, scratchy
or smooth?

Paper Hands

1. Fold the paper in half the long way. Tear it along this fold. Wrap a strip of paper around each hand, holding it in place with the thumb.

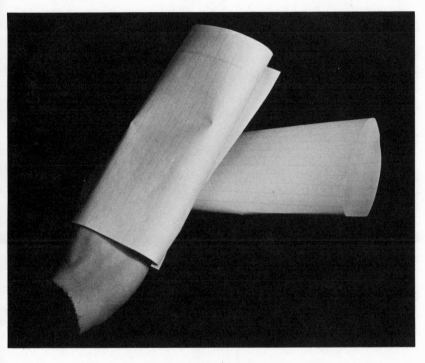

2. Have the child rub his hands together to produce a soft sound.

Variation: Aluminum foil or waxed paper may be used instead of plain paper.

Paper Plate Washboard

1. Have the child rub his fingernail along the edge to produce a sound. Compare the sound of the front fluted edge with the sound of the back fluted edge.

You will need: *1 paper plate with fluted edges*

Toilet Paper Tube Rhythm Sticks

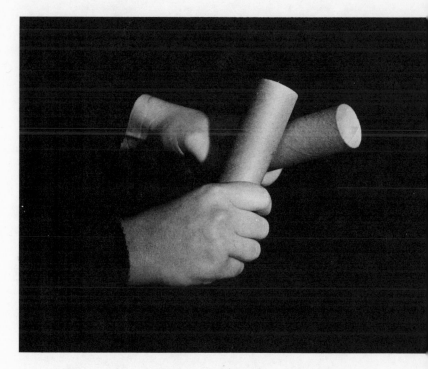

1. Have the child hit or rub the two tubes together to produce a hollow sound.

You will need: *2 toilet paper tubes or 2 paper towel tubes*

Paper Cups

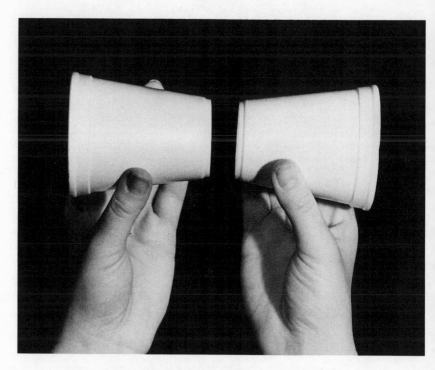

1. Have the child make different kinds of sounds with the cups by hitting the bottom ends together, hitting the open ends together, or by hitting the cups against a floor or table surface or against his body.

You will need: *2 paper or styrofoam cups*

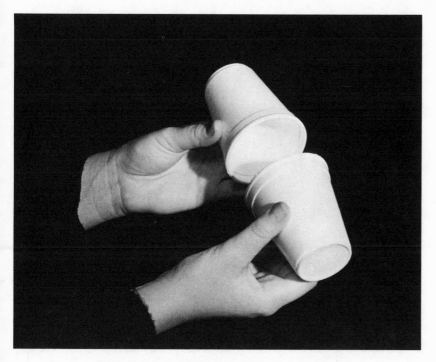

2. Combine the sounds into a rhythm pattern like the one below:
Count 1–2–3–4. On 1, have child hit bottom ends of cup on knees.
On 2, hit open ends together.
On 3, hit bottom ends together.
On 4, hit open ends together.
Repeat.

Paper Bag Maraca

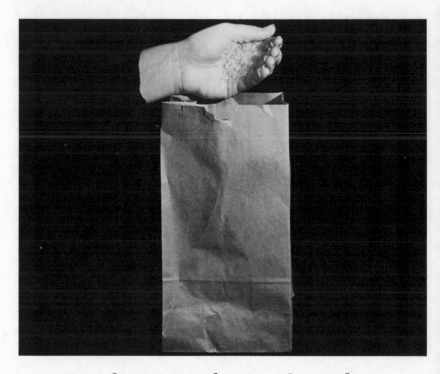

1. Pour the rice into the paper bag and twist the open end shut.

You will need: 1 paper bag
¼ cup of rice or corn kernels

2. Have the child hold the bag by the twisted end and shake it.

Pot and Pan Drums

1. Have the child use a wooden spoon or dowel to hit the bottoms of the pots and pans.

You will need: *Assortment of kitchen pots and pans*
1 wooden spoon or ½″ x 12″ dowel

2. Have the child line the pots and pans up from the smallest to the largest in size and listen for the tone differences. Help him notice which sound high or low, bright or dull. See what happens when he puts his hand on the pan right after he hits it.

Lid Cymbals

1. Have the child select a pair of "cymbals." Hold onto the handles and clang the two lids together.

You will need: 2 *pan lids*
2 *bacon presses*
2 *garbage can lids*

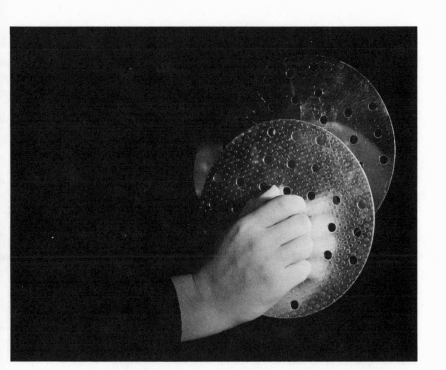

2. Compare the sounds made by the different sets of cymbals. Notice that a quieter sound can be made by gently brushing the cymbals against each other.

Brush and Screen

1. Have the child rub the brush up and down on the screen, creating different rhythm patterns.

You will need: 1 grease screen
                     1 wire brush

2. Vary the speed of the rubbing to create new rhythm patterns.

Brush Rhythm Variations

1. Have the child rub the vegetable brush against the sides of the grater. Each side of the grater will produce sounds in a different tempo. Rubbing the brush slower or faster will also create new sound patterns.

2. Have the child rub the vegetable brush across the surface of the strainer. Show him how to combine fast and slow movements with the vegetable brush to create new rhythm patterns.

You will need: 1 *cheese grater (4-sided)*
1 *strainer*
1 *vegetable brush*
1 *hairbrush*

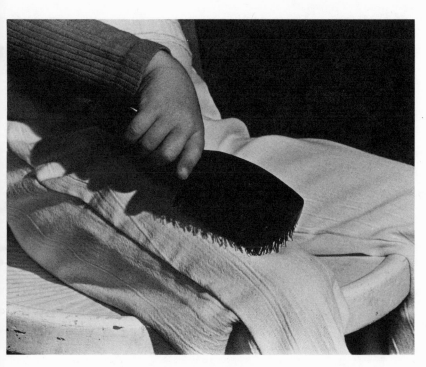

3. Have the child rub the hair brush on parts of his body clothing. Create rhythm patterns by moving the brush in different speeds or styles over the knee, arm, leg or stomach.

Measuring Cup Rhythms

1. Have the child hold one measuring cup by the handle and hit the bottom of it with a thimble.

2. Knuckles can also be used to hit the measuring cup.

You will need: 2 *metal measuring cups of the same size*
                           1 *thimble*
                           1 *½″ x 12″ dowel*

3. Also have the child use a dowel to hit the bottom or sides of the measuring cup to produce different sounds.

4. The two measuring cups may also be hit against each other. Rhythm patterns can be made by hitting either the bottoms or the open ends together in different combinations.

59

Washboard and Thimble

1. Washboard and thimble provide a fascinating sound-producer.

You will need: *1 washboard*
1 thimble

2. Have the child put the thimble on his forefinger. Ask him to rub it over the surface of the washboard to create a rhythm pattern.

Kitchen Spoons

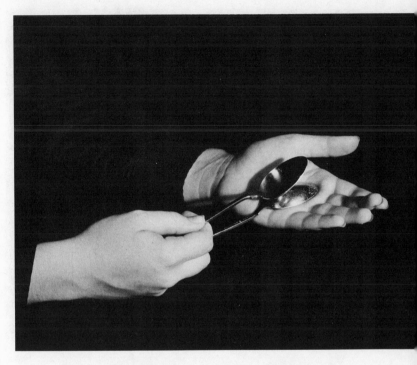

1. Have the child place one of the tea-spoons between his forefinger and middle finger and the other spoon between his forefinger and thumb with the spoon bottoms touching. Have him hold the teaspoons loosely, with the bottoms touching.

You will need: *2 stainless steel teaspoons*

2. The child can use the palm of the other hand to hit the teaspoons against each other to create a ringing sound. The spoons can also be struck against the leg, arm, head, etc.

Rhythm Stick Variations

1. Have the children make rhythm patterns by hitting two bolts together.

2. Hit two dowels together for a different kind of sound.

You will need: 2 *large bolts, approximately 12 inches long*
                    2 *1″ x 12″ dowels*
                    2 *wooden spoons*
                    1 *coffee pot stem*

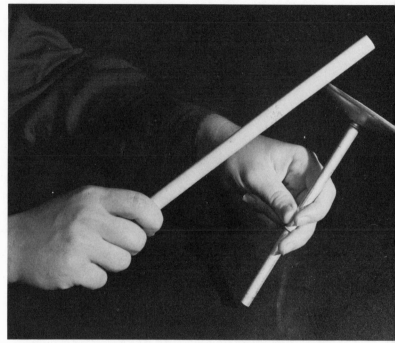

3. Two wooden spoons provide still another kind of rhythm sticks.

4. A dowel may be used to hit the coffee pot stem. Create different rhythms by pounding two items together in fast or slow tempos.

Rubber Ball Mallet

1. With the knife, make a hole for the dowel in the rubber ball.

You will need: 1 solid rubber ball
1 ½″ x 12″ dowel
1 kitchen knife
Glue

2. Put white glue into the hole and insert
the dowel. Allow the glue to dry before the mallet is used. Use the mallet
to hit drums, pots, pans, musical pipes
and other instruments.

Drum and Mallet Variations

 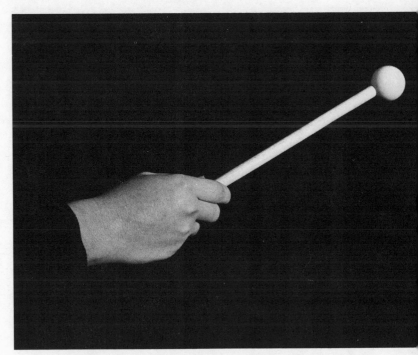

1. Fold the 3″ x 6″ piece of felt in half lengthwise. (Width will be 1½″.) Wrap the felt around one end of the dowel and secure it with the rubber band.

2. Another variation of a mallet uses the wooden bead and dowel. Insert the dowel into the hole in the bead and glue in place.

You will need: 2 ½″ x 12″ dowels
1 3″ x 6″ piece of felt
1 rubber band
1 1½″-diameter wooden bead

Assortment of gift boxes, shoe boxes, heavy cardboard boxes, cigar boxes, etc.

3. Have the child hit the boxes one at a time to hear the different sounds they produce. By alternating boxes and speeds of beating, a variety of rhythms can be produced.

Coffee Can Drum

1. Remove the plastic lid from the coffee can. With the hammer and nail, make two holes across from each other on the sides of the can.

2. Put several layers of tape over the holes to cover any sharp edges. With the nail, poke the hole through the tape.

You will need: 1 empty coffee can with plastic lid
1 nail
1 hammer
3' piece of cord
Masking tape

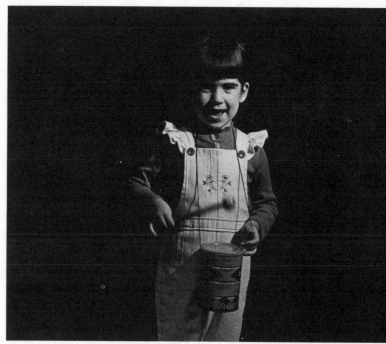

3. Thread the string through the holes and tie the ends together.

4. Replace the plastic lid. Slip the string over the child's head and the drum is ready to play with a mallet or his hand.

Ready-made Drums

The items in this list all make excellent ready-made drums for children to use.

You will need: 1 oatmeal box
1 ice cream carton
1 paint can
1 shortening can with
plastic lid

1 coffee can with both ends removed
and recovered with heavy paper,
plastic, or cloth
1 bucket with heavy paper, cloth, or plastic stretched over the opening

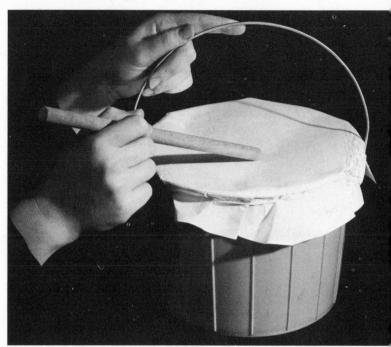

Tennis Ball Shaker

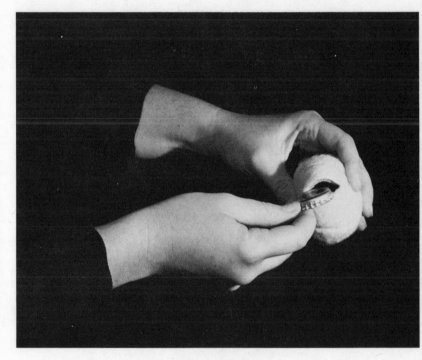

1. With the knife, cut a 1½″ slit in the tennis ball.

2. Squeeze the ball so the slit opens up, and put the four bottle caps inside.

You will need: 1 tennis ball
1 kitchen knife
4 bottle caps

3. Have the child hold the tennis ball in his hand and shake it. He may also roll it on the floor or bounce it for a soft shaking sound.

Box Rattles

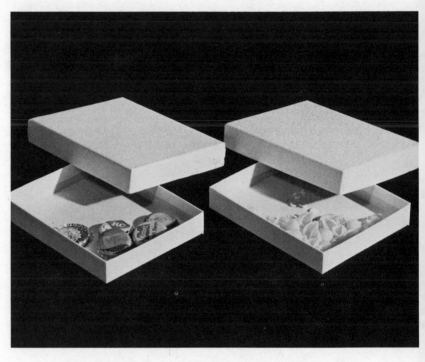

1. Fill the boxes with an assortment of the materials from the list above, and tape the lids shut.

You will need: *Several small gift boxes*
Some of the following sets of items; ¼ cup beans, rice,
or corn; 4 bells; 6 pebbles; ¼ cup sand; 6 bottle
caps; 4 erasers; 6 birthday candles; 4 washers; etc.
Masking tape

2. Have the children shake the boxes and
compare the different kinds of sounds.
For variation, try different combinations of sounds and rhythms.

Tin Shaker

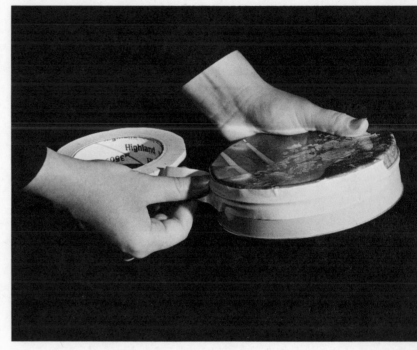

1. Fill the tin with the corn kernels.

2. Put the lid on and tape it shut.

You will need: 1 cookie or candy storage tin
½ cup corn kernels
Masking tape

3. Have the child hold the tin shaker in his hand. By varying the time between shakes, a variety of rhythm patterns can be produced.

Glass Shaker

1. Fill the jar with the corn kernels and secure the lid.

2. Tape the jar completely with masking tape to prevent it from shattering if it is dropped.

You will need: 1 *medium-size glass jar*
½ cup corn kernels, rice, beans, or macaroni
Masking tape

3. Have the child shake the jar while
   holding it in his hand. Varying the
   speeds of shaking will produce different rhythm patterns.

Pin Bottle Shaker

1. Stick the straight pins into the plastic jar about ½" to ¾" away from each other. Continue until the entire bottle is punctured with the pins.

2. Pour the rice into the bottle.

You will need:
   1 *medium size plastic bottle*
 100 *straight pins*
   ¼ *cup rice*
     Masking tape

3. Have the child look inside the bottle and try to imagine what kind of sound it will make. Then screw the lid on tightly and tape it down securely.

4. Have the child turn the bottle completely over and listen to the rice hit the pins until it reaches the bottom. Then he can flip the bottle over and listen to the sound repeat.

Toilet Paper Tube Shaker

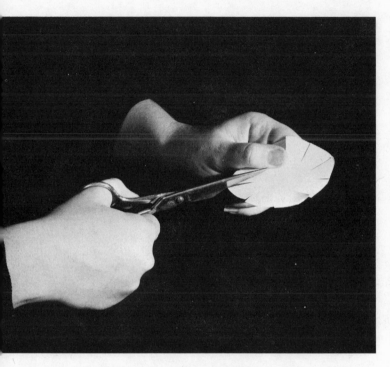

1. Cut two circles 2½″ in diameter out of the paper. Cut ½″ slits all the way around the circle about ½″ apart.

2. Glue one circle in place over one end of the toilet paper tube. Then fill the tube with the chosen material.

You will need: 1 toilet paper tube
1 piece of paper
Scissors
Glue
¼ cup rice, beans, corn, etc.

3. Glue the second circle in place over the open end.

4. Have the child play the shaker slow or fast as desired.

Plastic Lemon Maraca

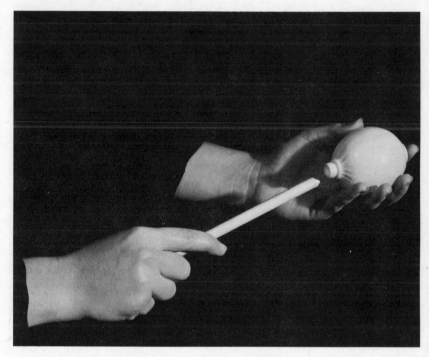

1. Put one of the materials from the list into the lemon.

2. Insert the dowel into the hole in the lemon.

You will need: 1 empty plastic lemon or lime with the squirter removed
1 12″ dowel of a diameter to fit the hole in the lemon
⅛ cup rice, sand, corn, etc.
Masking tape

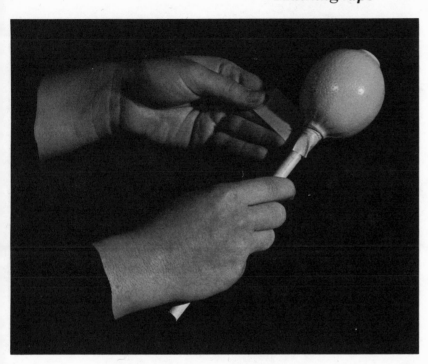

3. Tape the lemon in place.

4. Have the child use his hands to shake
the maraca in various rhythm patterns.

Gourd Maraca

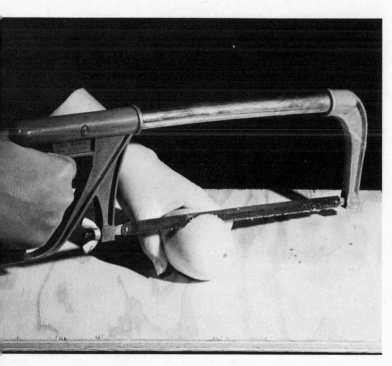

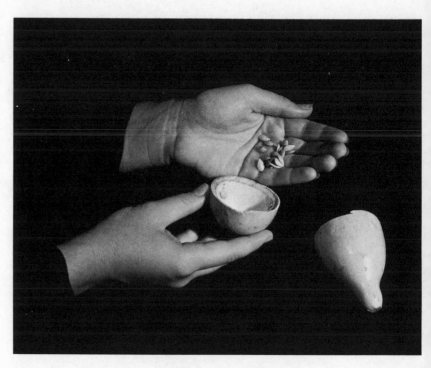

1. Saw off the top quarter of the gourd. Use a spoon to clean out the center of the gourd. Dry the hollowed gourd and seeds in a moderate oven for one hour, or until completely dry.

2. Put the seeds back into the gourd.

You will need: 1 *gourd*
1 *spoon*
1 *dish*
Masking tape
Saw

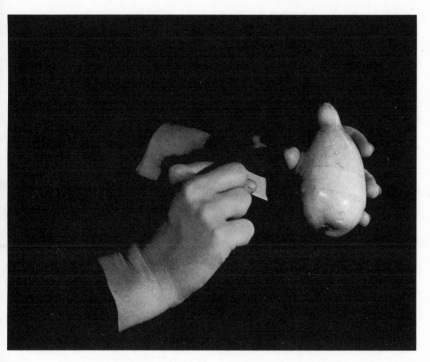

3. Tape the gourd back together.

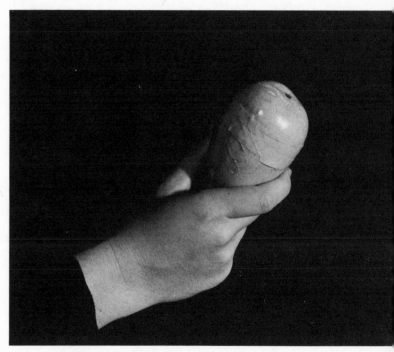

4. Have the child shake the gourd in his hand, varying the timing of his shakes to create rhythm patterns. The gourd is a soft-sounding maraca.

Toilet Bowl Float Shaker

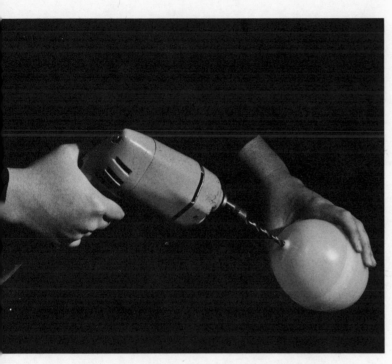

1. The threaded hole in the rod of the toilet bowl float does not reach the center. Drill the hole through the rod until it reaches the center.

2. Fill the float with the beebees.

You will need: 1 *toilet bowl float (available at hardware stores)*
                   20 *beebees*
                    1 *long bolt to fit the threading in the rod of the*
                            toilet bowl float
                     Electric drill

 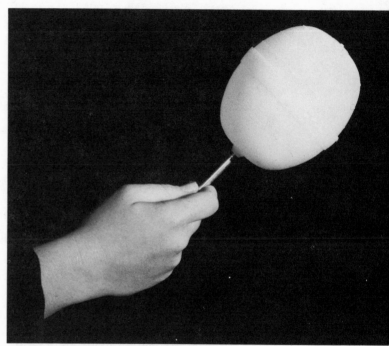

3. Screw the bolt securely into the rod for the handle.

4. This is another hand shaker instrument which can produce various rhythm patterns depending on how it is shaken.

Tin Can Tubo

1. Put the rice into the can without the lid and the bottle caps into the can with the lid.

2. Push the lid down to close it.

You will need: 2 empty tin cans of the same size
                        (keep the lid on one can)
                      ¼ cup rice
                      4 bottle caps
                        Masking tape

3. Tape the two cans together with masking tape.

4. Have the child shake the tin can tubo with his hands and listen to the two contrasting sounds coming from within.

Tin Can Bell

1. Tie the washer securely to the center of the string.

2. With the hammer and nail, punch a hole in the center of the can.

You will need: 1   *small tin can*
                                 1   *1" washer*
                                   1   *12" piece of string*
                                   1   *5" nail*
                                       Hammer

3. Thread the string with the washer through the can, making sure the washer hangs low enough to hit the bottom edge of the can. Retie the string so it cannot slip out of the can.

4. Have the child hold the top edge of the tin can bell and ring it.

Horseshoe Triangle

1. Tie the string to the middle of the horseshoe. Hold the horseshoe by the string and strike it with the nail.

You will need: 1 horseshoe
                                1 8″ piece of string
                                1 5″ nail

Jingle Bells

1. Hammer the nail into the top of the dowel. Tie a bell on each end of the 8″ and 12″ pieces of string. Tie the center of these strings to the nail and glue in place.

You will need:

1 1″ x 12″ dowel or 1″ x 1″ x 12″ piece of wood	1 12″ piece of string
1 2″ nail	1 8″ piece of string
4 bells	Glue

2. Have the child shake the stick and he will hear the bell jingling and knocking against the dowel.

Jingle Pole

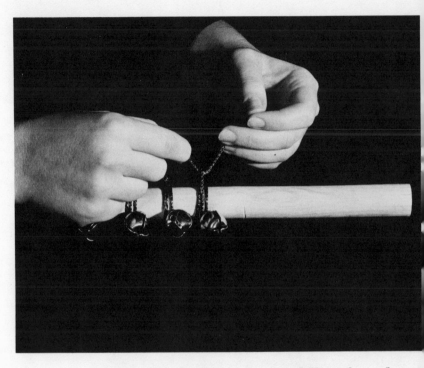

1. Tie one bell in the middle of each piece of string. Tie each bell around the dowel at about 1″ intervals.

You will need: 1 *1″ x 12″ dowel*
4 *bells*
4 *10″ pieces of string*
Glue

2. Glue the bells in place. Have the child shake the dowel to create the jingle bell sound.

String Wrist or Ankle Ringer

1. Tie the bells onto the string at about 1″ intervals, leaving about 2″ at each end for tying.

You will need: 1 8″ piece of cotton cord or elastic
                     5 bells

2. Tie the string of bells around the wrist
   or ankle and shake.

Felt Wrist or Ankle Ringer

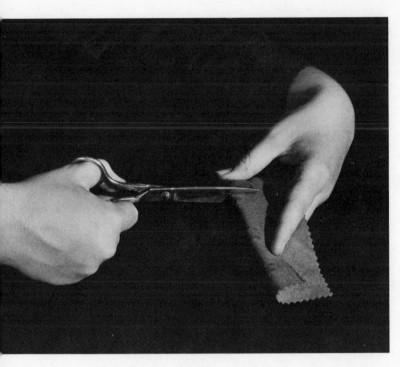

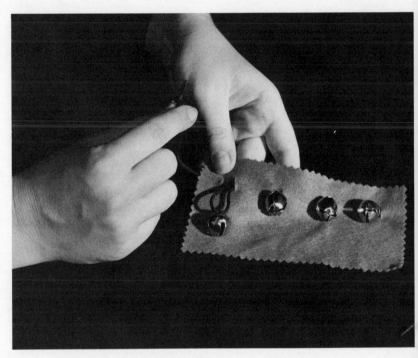

1. Fold the 6″ edge of the felt rectangle a quarter of the way up. On the fold make four sets of slits placed evenly along the band.

2. Weave the shoe lace up and down through the slits, stringing the bells with it.

You will need:
1 3" x 6" piece of felt
4 bells
1 nylon shoelace
Glue
Scissors

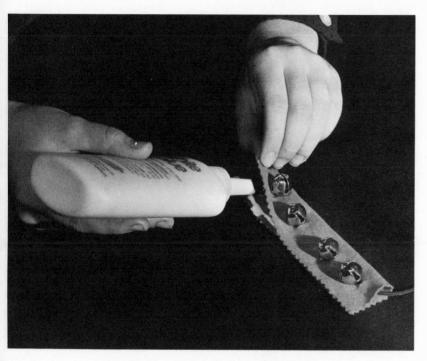

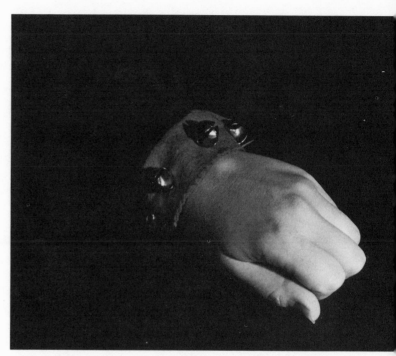

3. Fold the felt in half lengthwise and glue the 6" edges together.

4. Have the child tie the band to his wrist or ankle and shake.

Leather Wrist or Ankle Ringer

1. With the hammer and nail, make two holes at one end of the piece of leather. Make three more holes spaced evenly over the rest of the strip. Overlap the ends of the leather and mark the position of the two holes on the mating end. Punch out the holes with the hammer and nail.

2. Thread a bell on each piece of string. Thread the string down through one of the single holes and tie the string around the leather strap. Repeat this for the other two holes.

You will need: 1 ¾″ x 10″ piece of leather
1 4″ nail
4 5″ pieces of yarn or string
4 bells
Hammer

3. Overlap the ends of the band so that it makes a circle. Line up the two sets of holes and thread the string through them. This will serve as the opening for the child's foot or hand to pass through. When the child has the band on his ankle or wrist, have him tie it in place and shake.

Wood Tambourine

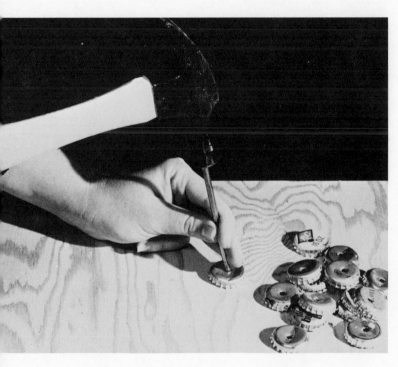

1. With the hammer and large nail, punch holes in the middle of all the bottle caps.

2. Thread four bottle caps on each of the four 2½″ nails.

You will need: 1 1″ x 2″ x 10″ piece of wood
16 bottle caps (remove cork from center if necessary)
1 5″ nail
4 2½″ nails
Hammer

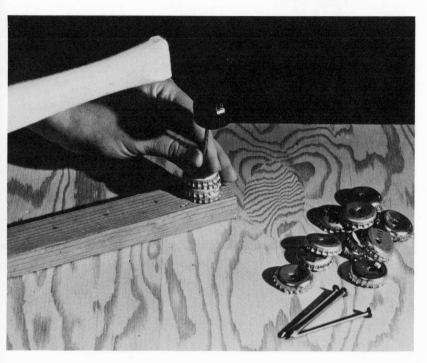

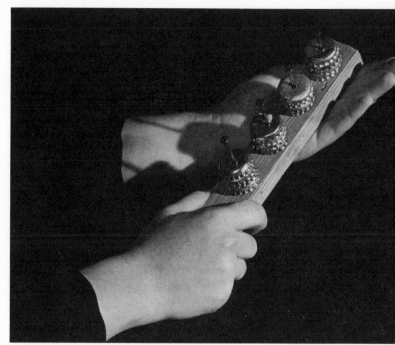

3. Hammer the four nails with bottle caps in the wood at 2″ intervals, leaving about 3″ at one end for a handle.

4. Have the child play the wood tambourine by shaking it in the air, against the palm of his free hand, or against other parts of his body.

Embroidery Hoop Tambourine

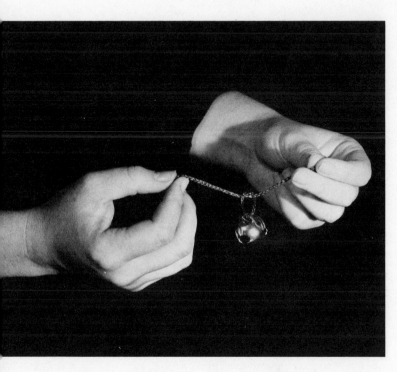

1. Tie one bell in the middle of each piece of string.

2. Tie each bell to the embroidery hoop, leaving space for the child to place his hand.

You will need: 6 bells
6 5" pieces of string
1 wood or metal embroidery hoop
Glue

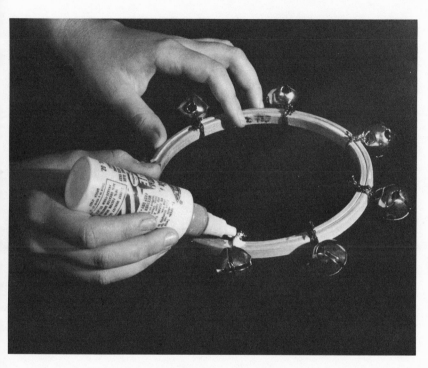

3. Glue all the bells in place.

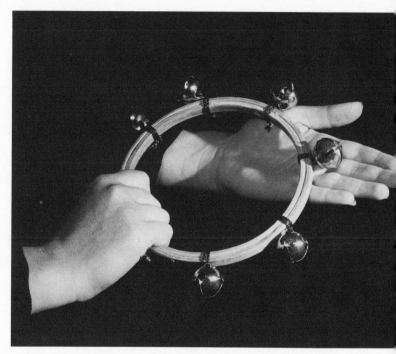

4. Have the child shake the tambourine or hit it against the palm of his hand or other parts of his body.

Pie Tin Tambourine

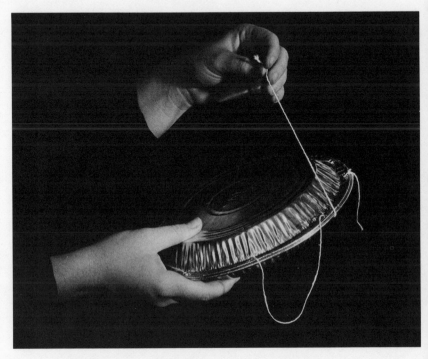

1. Put the two pie tins together with the open sides together. With a nail, poke nine holes around the rim of the pie tins.

2. Attach the two pie tins together by weaving a long piece of string through the holes.

You will need: 2 *aluminum foil pie tins*
18 *bottle caps (remove cork if necessary)*
String
Nail
Hammer

3. With the hammer and nail, make holes in the center of the bottle caps. Thread three bottle caps onto a string and thread this through a pair of holes in the pie tins.

4. Repeat this five times, leaving three holes without any bottle caps, so the child will have a place for his hand. Have the child shake the tambourine or tap it against the palm of his hand or leg.

Embroidery Hoop Shaker

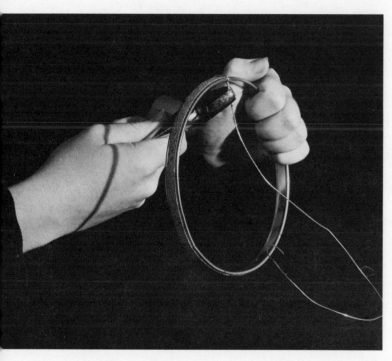 

1. Separate the parts of the embroidery hoop. With the pliers, twist a piece of wire around the middle of the inside hoop.

2. With the hammer and nail, make holes in the center of the bottle caps. Thread six bottle caps onto the wire.

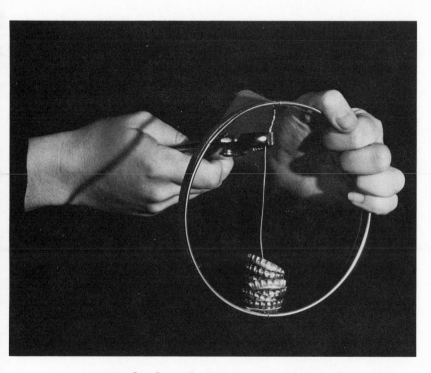 

3. With the pliers, secure the loose end of the wire to the hoop. Repeat steps 1–3 two more times. Place the two other wires on each side of the center one.

4. Secure the outside hoop over the inside hoop and have the child shake it.

Finger Castanets

1. With the hammer and nail, punch two holes in each bottle cap. Thread a piece of elastic through the holes and knot the ends inside the top. Slip the bottle caps on the child's thumb and forefinger and clap them together.

2. For a variation, use buttons with elastic threaded through the two holes and tied at the top. These are also worn on the child's forefinger and thumb. Clap the two together.

You will need: 2 *bottle caps*
                                 Elastic
                                 Nail
                                 Hammer

3. Use small jar lids with two holes in the center and elastic threaded through the holes and tied. Wear and use the same way.

4. Use walnut shells with tape handles. Hit together by using the same fingers.

Pie Pan Cymbals

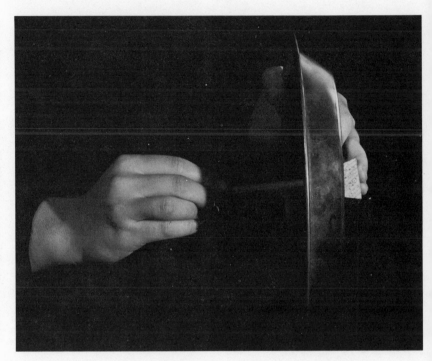

1. Punch one or two holes in the center of each pie pan depending on the type of knob being used.

2. If using the blocks of wood, use a pencil to mark where the screws should go in each block.

You will need: 2 *metal pie pans*
                         2 *drawer knobs and ½-*
                              inch screws or two
                              1″ x 1″ x 1″ cubes
                              of wood

Hammer
Nail
Pencil
Screwdriver

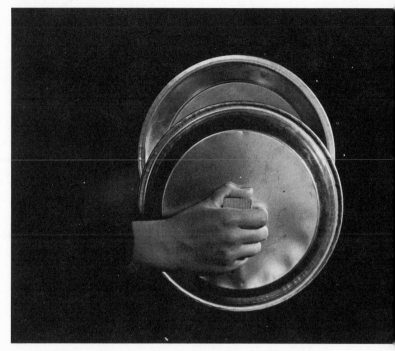

3. Screw the knobs or blocks of wood onto the pie pan with the screwdriver.

4. Have the child hold the knobs and bang the cymbals together for a loud sound or brush them together for a softer sound.

Foil Cymbals

1. With the nail, poke two holes in the center of each pie tin about 3″ apart. Thread elastic through the holes and tie. Have the child slip his hands through the elastic and bang the tins together.

You will need: 2 aluminum foil pie tins
2 6″ pieces of elastic
Nail

Sandpaper Hands

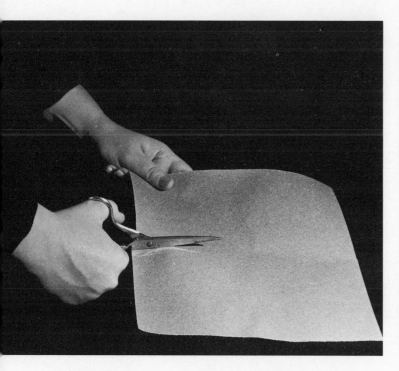

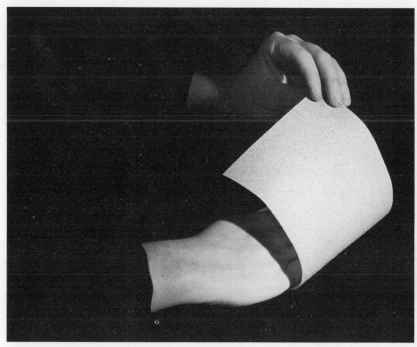

1. Fold the sandpaper in half the long way and cut it along this fold.

2. Wrap a strip of sandpaper around each hand.

You will need: *1 sheet of sandpaper*

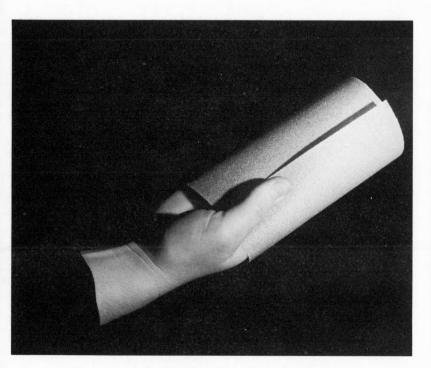

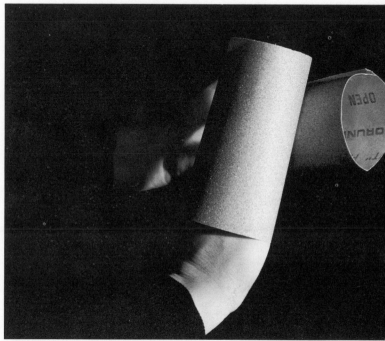

3. Hold it in place with the thumb.

4. Have the child rub his hands together to produce a scratching sound.

Sandpaper Rhythm Sticks

1. Measure and cut two pieces of sandpaper to fit around each one of the dowels. Wrap one piece of sandpaper around each dowel. Glue down the edges of the sandpaper and thumbtack it into place.

You will need: 1 piece of sandpaper
2 1" x 12" dowels
8 thumbtacks
Glue
Ruler

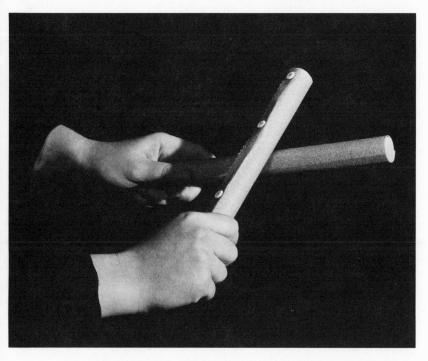

2. Have the child rub the two sticks together to produce a scratching noise.

Rasps

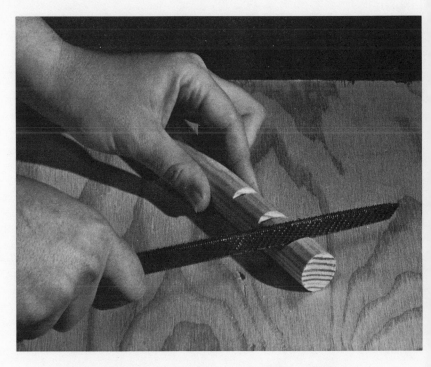

1. File five grooves into one side of the large dowel. Beginning 1″ from the top of the dowel, place the grooves 1″ apart. Make them ¼″ deep.

You will need: 1 1″ x 12″ dowel
1 ½″ x 12″ dowel
1 wood file

2. Have the child hold the grooved
dowel in one hand and the plain dowel
in the other. Rub the plain dowel
across the grooves and listen to the
razorlike noise.

Sandpaper Blocks

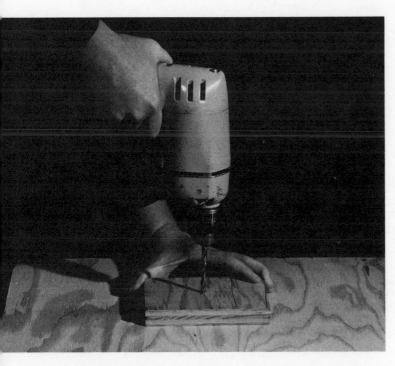

1. Drill a hole ½″ in diameter through the center of each piece of wood. You may want to countersink the holes on one side so the screw heads will lie flush with the block.

2. Screw on the knob with the screw-driver.

You will need: 2 3½" x 5" x ¾" pieces of wood   Electric drill
2 drawer knobs and 1" screw   Screwdriver
1 sheet of sandpaper   Scissors
12 thumbtacks

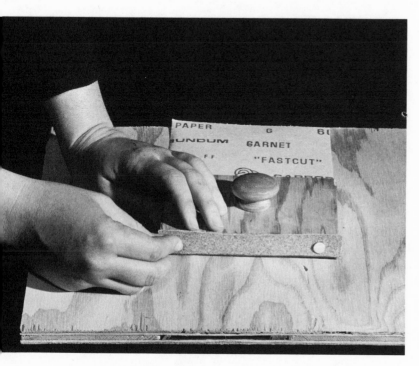

3. Cut the sandpaper so it will cover two edges and the bottom of the block. Thumbtack the sandpaper to the edges to keep it in place.

4. Have the child hold the knobs and rub the blocks together to produce a scratching sound.

Coconut Horse's Hooves

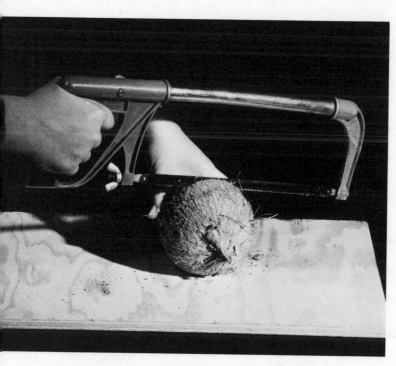 

1. Begin to saw the coconut in half, stopping when the milk starts to drain out. Pour the milk into the bowl. Then finish cutting the coconut.

2. Clean out the coconut meat with a kitchen knife.

You will need: 1 coconut
Saw
Bowl
Sandpaper
Kitchen knife

3. Sand the outside of the coconut until it is smooth.

4. Have the child take a coconut half in each hand and hold them together. Try tapping them with the halves centered and again with them off center.

Rhythm Box

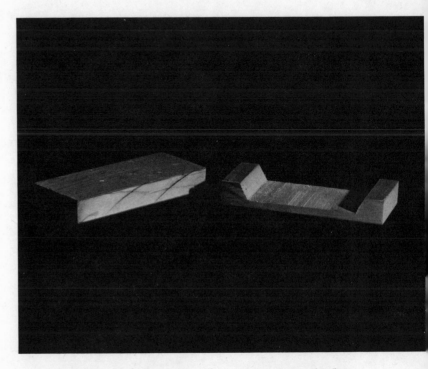

1. With the band saw, cut one of the blocks of wood into the shape shown on the right in the photograph above. The cut should start and end about one inch from the end of the block and should remove about half the thickness of the wood.

You will need: 2 1" x 3" x 5" blocks of wood
                   1 ½" x 12" dowel
                   Band saw
                   Glue

2. Glue the two blocks together, leaving
   a hollow space between them. With
   the dowel, strike the "box" to produce
   a hollow sound.

Musical Instruments

Toilet Paper Tube Kazoo

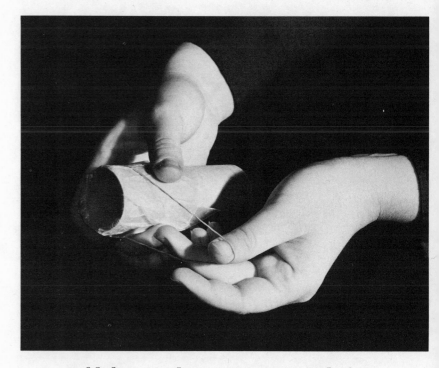

1. Fold the waxed paper over one end of the toilet paper tube and secure it with a rubber band.

You will need: *1 4″ x 4″ piece of waxed paper*
Toilet paper tube
Rubber band
Paper punch

2. Have the child place the open end of the tube close to his mouth and hum into it to produce a buzzing sound. If you have a problem keeping the waxed paper on the toilet paper roll, make an air-release hole with the paper punch about 1″ from the end of the tube nearest the waxed paper.

Beast Screamer

1. Cut the straws into varied lengths of 3, 5, and 7 inches. Use the scissors handle to flatten 1″ of each straw at one end.

2. Cut the flattened end diagonally into a point.

You will need: 2 *plastic straws*
Scissors

3. Have the child place the straw with the pointed end on top of his tongue and blow.

4. Listen to the screaming noise the instrument makes. Because of their varied lengths, the straws will produce sounds of different pitches.

Comb Kazoo

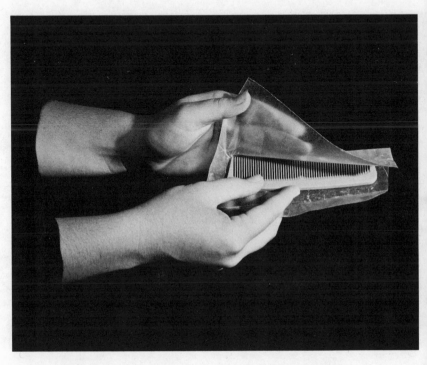

1. Fold the piece of waxed paper in half and place the fold over the teeth of the comb.

You will need: 1 *comb*
1 *piece of waxed paper, the same length*
and twice as wide as the comb

2. Hold the back of the comb and wax paper, while the lips rest on the teeth of the comb. Hum a tune and move the combs from side to side to produce different sounds.

Plastic Tube Harmonica

1. Cut the tubing into 2″, 3″, 4″, 5″, and 6″ lengths. Place a piece of masking tape over one end of each piece of tubing. Have the child place his lower lip on the side of the tube and blow into the open end of the tube to produce a whistle sound.

2. Now tape the tubes together according to size. Have the child blow into the tubes as he slides them sideways in front of his mouth. This will produce different pitches the same way a harmonica does.

Rubber Band Zither

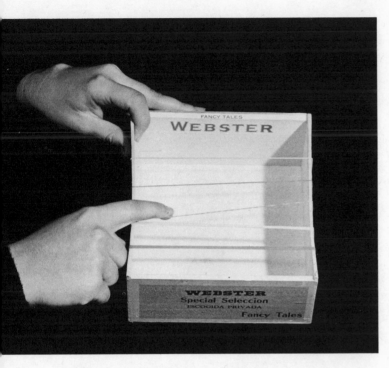

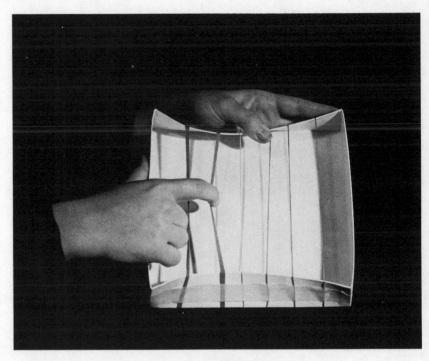

1. Slip several rubber bands of varying size and thickness over each lid and the box and tape them in place.

2. The rubber bands should be spaced evenly across the lid or box.

You will need: 1   lid of a gift box
1   cigar box
1   candy-tin lid
    Assortment of rubber bands
    Masking tape

3. Have the child strum the instrument
   with his fingers.

Musical Jars

1. Fill the jars with varied depths of water. Line the jars up according to the amount of water in them, from the least to the most. Have the child hit the jars with the nail and listen to the differences in pitch. By playing the jars in different orders, the child can create his own tune.

You will need: 6 jars of the same size
                           1 5″ nail
                              Water

Bottle Blowing

1. Fill one bottle half full of water and another bottle three-quarters full. Have the children blow into the bottles and listen to the differences in pitch. Children can also create their own songs by blowing into the bottles in turn.

You will need: 3 soda-pop bottles of the same size
Water

2. Three bottles of different sizes can be
used to produce different pitches.

Shell Chime

1. Tie one or two shells on separate pieces of string and then onto the piece of driftwood. Attach the strings to the wood at about 1″ intervals. Glue the shells and strings in place. The shells need to hit one another to produce a tinkling sound. The shell chime can be placed outside in the wind or played by hand.

You will need: 20 shells of various sizes
        1 piece of driftwood
         String
         Scissors
         Glue

Nail Chime

1. Tie one or two nails onto a piece of string. Attach the string to the embroidery hoop and glue in place. Repeat this with strings spaced 1″ apart until the hoop is covered. The nail chime may be played with the child's hand or hung outside to play in the wind.

You will need: 1 embroidery hoop
30 nails of assorted sizes
String
Glue

Musical Bolt Chime

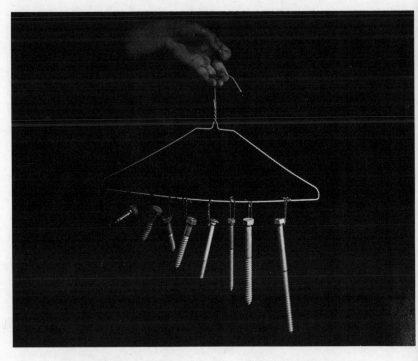

1. Hang the bolts from the clothes hanger with pieces of string, arranging from small to large. Glue the bolts and strings in place. The child may use his hands or a dowel to hit the bolts and make music. The bolt chime may also be used as a wind chime.

You will need: 1   clothes hanger
                                  1   ½″ x 12″ dowel
                                      Large bolts in an assortment of sizes
                                      Glue

Musical Pipes

1. With a short length of wire, hang each pipe from the broom handle or wooden stand. Arrange the pipes according to size. If using the broom handle, rest it on the seats of two chairs. The child may use a dowel, his hand, or a nail to hit the pipes. The pipes can be played all at once or one at a time.

You will need: Water pipe in an assortment of lengths
Wire
Wooden stand or two chairs and a broom handle
1 ½″ x 12″ dowel
1 5″ nail

Rubber Band Strings

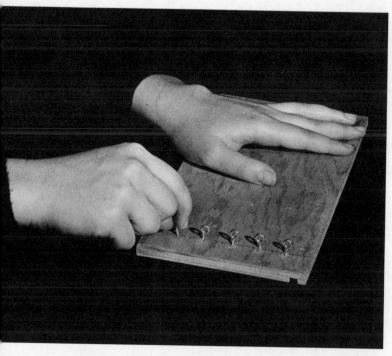

1. Draw a straight line 1″ from the 8″ edge (top) of the wood. On this line, screw in five hooks, evenly spaced. Hammer the hooks slightly into the wood before screwing.

2. Draw a second line from the mid point of the right side to the lower left hand corner. Screw in five hooks on this line. Each hook should be directly below a corresponding hook on the top line.

You will need: 1 piece of wood, ½" x 8" x 12"
10 screw-eyes or nails
5 rubber bands of the same size

Hammer
Pencil
Ruler

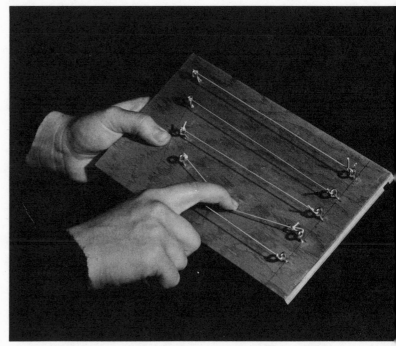

3. Loop or tie the rubber bands over the hooks.

4. Have the child strum the rubber bands one at a time or all together to produce a tune. Try placing the instrument on top of a variety of boxes, to hear how this changes the tone quality. A tin storage can, a wastebasket or other objects of convenient size should provide interesting contrasts.